The Art Of Pitching

Denny McLain

Edited by Thomas Saunders

Copyright © 2013 Glendower Media

All rights reserved.

ISBN-978-0-914303-10-7

www.glendowermedia.com

P O Box 661
Whitmore Lake, Michigan 48189

Dedication

Denny McLain

I want to thank all who have made my career what it was and has been.

I want to thank my Dad and Mom for all their help. Although it was tough love, he showed me what determination and education was all about and how importantly both contributed to people's success. My Dad in my younger years spent hour after hour teaching me the fundamentals of pitching and the most important fundamental, "throwing Strikes". I want to thank my parents for running me from game to game, school to school, ballpark the ballpark. And I want to thank all of those coaches and all of those parents who after my dad died were there for me to continue playing the game that I love so much. To all of you I say thank you, thank you, thank you.

My High School Coach Carmelite Priest, Father Austin Coupe, who taught me about competing and understanding that the game was more than just hitting and pitching. Then there are the following major leaguers who made my pitching career possible, taking a chance on a crazy looking guy wearing glasses. Charley Dressen ,the great Dodger manager and finally our Tiger manager, when he called me up to the Tigers in September of 1963 and after watching me pitch my first game said to me: "You are a right handed sandy Koufax, lots of control issues but with as good of stuff that I ever saw". Then Mayo Smith and Johnny Sain. Johnny made me a complete pitcher and taught me the toughest side of the game, "mental". Johnny always told me and taught me how to see each and every pitch before I threw it to a hitter, and he and Hal Naragon, a man who never gets the credit he deserves, for working with me tirelessly, and forever it seemed, until I developed a slider that had the effect of sliding and sinking at the same time. A real "out" pitch that made me almost unhittable for a couple years. There have been numerous others including hitters like Al Kaline who would talk to me about what hitters would look for in certain situations against me. When you get that kind of help from one of the game's greatest of all time, you can't hardly lose if you stay healthy.

And those of you whom I have missed I am sorry. I could write a book on the things so many taught me and how they supported me. No one wins baseball games as a pitcher by himself in any form. It takes more than the 8 guys on the field. Many hours and many supporters gave me priceless information and help with all that it took to have some success in the great game of major league baseball.

I leave you also with this thought, all you folks who want to be Major League Pitchers. Please, I beseech you, to first always think about an education. In today's game they want smart guys, guys that can comprehend and guys who want it badly. Keep this in mind; you can still be good enough to be able to receive a college education because of baseball. That is if you are a pretty good player with good grades, you have a great chance of some kind of scholarship for sports or otherwise. But first and always think education.

The Art Of Pitching

CONTENTS

1	Pitching	Page 1
2	Sizing Up The Batters	Page 31
3	That Extra Pitch	Page 40
4	Playing A Ball Game	Page 48
5	Equipment and Exercise	Page 63
6	Talent & Fast Balls	Page 66

TIPS & APPLICATIONS
"LISTEN & PAY ATTENTION"

Ever wondered what it looked like building greatness?
 Start from the beginning and that is what we are doing with this book of instruction and stories of how we perfected certain pitches and applications.

We always see the end product but never really know what it took to get there.

That's why I am excited to share with you my most popular series of tips and applications for making you a better pitcher.

Our Pitchers with our Detroit Tigers, myself included, worked very hard.   There is no replacement for working hard and trying to understand the issue that you are dealing with.
By breaking everything down, one movement at a time, it simplifies the pitcher's ability to understand. From the very first moment you step on the mound you are learning your body and its ability to deliver that pitch or pitches that we need to be successful.

Light up our minds right on the field. Treat every throwing session as a classroom, making mental notes and otherwise for you to understand. And one thing; practice, practice and practice.
You don't have to throw a pitch every time that you work on your footing, positioning, weight balance,

weight movement, and leg positions. Sooner than later all of those working parts do come together.

These are tips and bits of information that make you a better pitcher. I guarantee you one thing; these tips of information will make you a much better pitcher, maybe not someone who will be in the Major Leagues but you will be more than competitive when you take the mound and nothing happens overnight.

It took me more than 18 months to learn the right and proper way to throw a slider and my slider wound up allowing me to throw other pitches with the same grips and positioning myself on the mound.

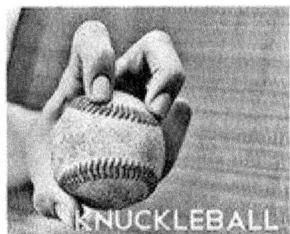

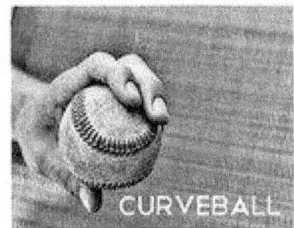

Chapter 1

Pitching

Denny McLain

There are still some managers who believe that all pitchers must be big guys. Big fellows, it is true, are more likely to have the strength of the arm and back that a big league pitcher needs. But still there have been plenty of good pitchers in the history of baseball who have been short, or skinny, or both.

You do however need a strong arm and you make your arm strong by throwing. Every successful pitcher I ever knew started by throwing when he was young and did a lot of it. You don't necessarily have to throw baseballs all the time. Some kids started by throwing rocks. But one thing is certain: *They always threw at a target.* The name of the game is control, control, control. Even with mediocre to poor stuff people can get hitters out if they can throw strikes. Now that doesn't mean you take every hitter to three balls and two strikes but it does mean you concentrate and try to hit some corners. But you don't have to hit it on the eighth of an inch of the corner, just get a good solid inch or two. Remember, no hitter as ever hit 1000 and only one formidable hitter in the modern era has hit 400, that being Ted Williams, may be the greatest hitter of all time.

One of the first rules for developing a pitching arm: Always throw at a target. Another good rule is this: Always take a step when you throw. If you do that, you will develop an easy motion that gets the body into the pitch and does not put such a strain on the arm. That is, do not bring the ball back beside your ear, of just behind your shoulder and start your throw with a bent arm. Reach away back until your arm is fully extended. Then, with your eye on the target, step forward and throw the ball.

Never just play catch to play catch; always have some kind of an idea of what you are trying to do. Work on something all the time not necessarily a fastball, but at least throw that pitch for a strike. Don't worry about speed just worry about strikes. Again, no one has ever hit 1000. There is one exceptional exercise that one can do and give them a little bit of rhythm and to find their natural throwing position. In other words, take a running start and then go ahead and throw the ball hard down 60, 70, 80, 90 or 100 feet. This exercise will give you some rhythm it will make you keep your head on straight and it will give you a target to throw to all the time. Again work on what you are throwing to.

Even when you are just playing catch, or just fooling around, follow those rules. Pick out a target and throw at it. Throw with the full length of your arm. Step when you throw. When you are "fooling around" or playing catch is when you develop your throwing habits. Make sure they are good habits.

The next step in making yourself into a pitcher is to learn to make the ball go where you want it to go. Pitchers nowadays are going to find it harder to do that, because the strike zone has been made smaller. Instead of getting the ball under the shoulders, you must now get it lower than the batter's arm-pits. Control, therefore, is becoming ever more important.

You learn control by practice, of course. But you do not practice merely aiming the ball. The good pitcher does not *aim* the ball, in the ordinary sense, at all. He keeps his eye on the target and thrown full strength. Practice allows him to make the adjustments needed to bring the ball to the strike zone. I would far rather see young pitcher throwing the ball two feet over the catcher's head- with full length and full strength of arm- than see him cutting down on his speed and cramping his arm to "steer" the ball. So get your eye on a target- the knee or the thigh of the catcher, for instance, and let it fly. If you miss, keep trying to bring the ball up or down, depending where it went. But don't start to get cozy with your pitches. Let the ball fly!

The first sort of control you must get is the up-and-down control. If you learn to get the ball below the batter's belt and keep throwing it there, you will find it relatively easy to get it over the plate. As a matter of fact, once you have learned to keep the ball low, you are already half a pitcher. It is a rare batter indeed who can consistently drive a low pitch any distance. The home runs and the fence-rattlers- the doubles and triples- almost always come off high pitches. If you keep the ball low, you will keep the score low.

But let me stop right here to remind you of something every athlete should know: You must warm up before you use the full strength of any muscle. Getting warm normally took me 10 to 15 minutes depending upon the weather to really get loose enough that I was willing to let the ball go. Now warming up does not mean that you go full bore to the wall. You walk it up, you take your time, you mix in other pitches, you look at the movement of every pitch that you throw and make sure that you are still working on control. No matter what the weather is like, even if it is a ninety-degree day in July, get your arm warmed up before you throw. Always start with a few easy throws and take a few off-speed throws before you begin to bear down. About fifteen throws should do it. If the weather is cold and the perspiration does not start, maybe you'll need twenty-five throws. Make sure you have some sweat flowing before you let the ball go, most injuries will occur if you are not loose and ready to throw the ball. The boys with the sore arms and the boys who burn themselves out early are the ones who scorn this simple precaution, who start to fire full strength before they have warmed up and loosened the muscles. They may get away with it for a while- even a season or two. Then one day they wake up with a sore arm that will not go away. And too often-if they do not have a smart doctor to help them- they may see the strength drain right out of the arm, for good. So take these warm up pitches, no matter how boring they may seem, and no matter what the temptation may be to show the spectators what a strong arm you have. You owe it to your arm to give it a chance to avoid injury.

Now I do not mean to suggest that you must coddle your arm. But I do mean you must take care of it; you must treat it like it's the only arm that you have to throw pitches and keep at this in mind it is the only arm that you have to be a pitcher and be effective and to hope with the proper training and the proper support you become a professional pitcher. On the contrary I think you should throw full strength and throw often, in order to develop your throwing muscles. The boy who "saves" his arm for the day when he pitches in a game is like the miser who fails to invest his money. He may discover some day it has lost much of its value. You have to keep muscles working full strength to keep them strong and let them get stronger. This means throwing every day (except the day after you have pitched a full game) and throwing until you begin to feel the effects of the effort. When I pitched I threw the ball every day starting with the first day of spring training. Now that does not mean I went out and through line drives to the catcher on the first day. I took my time. I established a routine and one pitch at a time, I learned something about myself. An example of what I did was the following; on the first day I would throw about 10 minutes, on the second day I would throw up to 20 minutes, on the

The Art Of Pitching

third day I would throw 5 to 7 minutes and then when I was pitching as we pitched every fourth day it was time to let it go. The game today has changed dramatically meaning that pitchers will pitch 5 to 6 innings and only have to pitch every fifth to six day. Unless you are the ace, then that ace will pitch his regular turn every fifth day in most cases.

You are going to hear this from me a lot, control, control, control and more control. Always be working on something and that something should always be control especially when you are just playing catch.

Before we get into grips, curveballs, sliders and the rest of it, I want to emphasize about pitching and pitching at certain age levels. If you are a pitcher in Little League let's say 11 or 12 years old, you should be able to get out every hitter in your league with a fastball. That means no sliders, no curveballs, nothing that makes you spend or apply your arm in an unorthodox manner, so that only leaves us with three pitches; fastball, changeup and fork ball. We will discuss all of these pitches but I want to tell you one more time that the fastball is the pitch. The fastball is your number one weapon at all times. If you can't get out hitters with your fastball in your age group then you probably are not going to play professional baseball. If you need a curveball, slider, or a screwball then you are in trouble as far as professional baseball goes. Additionally your arm is not physically able to handle that kind of pressure. Arms have lots of vulnerability. We're talking rotator cuffs, we're talking elbows, we're talking wrists, and we're talking, certainly, the right positions to release the ball. But if we are throwing a good fastball we are more than likely throwing that fastball from the appropriate and proper position. You do not need again, one more time, a curveball, slider, or anything else that would be considered junk. There are a lot of people out there, coaches who mean well but do have a tendency in the heat of the moment to put winning ahead of doing some harm to a young pitcher. Nothing is worth hurting or harming a young arm from the age of 10 to 18. Yes I said 18. There are very few people in the game of baseball at any level including major leaguers who really understand and are able to master a curveball, slider, or other junk pitches that can be effective. Nothing makes me more upset than watching the Little League World Series and seeing pitchers of 11 and 12 years old throwing curveballs and sliders or at least what they think are sliders and curveballs. What they really are is sloppy slopped breaking balls that do nothing but extend the arm in such a manner that it can cause serious harm. These pitches are death for a young pitcher. Remember your arm has to develop before you are strong enough, before your tendons are strong enough and your rotator cuff is strong enough to withstand the pressure of these breaking balls.

The Art Of Pitching

Once you have learned how to get the ball into the strike zone- and into the lower part of the strike zone- you can begin to think about pitches. As a matter of fact, if you have learned control and have good speed, you have already got the best pitch you'll ever have- a

Hold your fast ball with your fingertips across the seams.

good fast ball. In most leagues it is still the number one pitch, the Old Reliable, the best way to get a batter out. 80 to 85% of my pitches, believe it or not, were fastballs. Why did I throw so many fastballs? Because number one, I had a good one and number two God blessed me with great control. I could hit the black 90% of the time of home plate. Now look at a home plate and see what the black looks like it is small, teeny and in some cases minute. While I struck out a lot of guys, I struck out most of them with a fastball. Probably 30% of my strikeouts were strikeouts when the hitter took the pitch for strike three. There is nothing greater in the game of baseball than a fastball pitcher with great control or just common good control when it counts. I never tried to hit the black on home plate when I was either winning or nearly tied in a ballgame. Challenging the hitter is what the game is all about and we will talk about challenging hitters later.

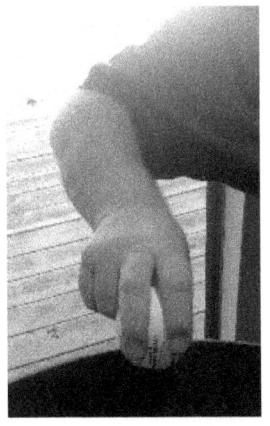
You make your best pitch more effective however by learning to throw other pitches. The number two pitch is the curve ball, the ball that "breaks" out of a straight line and dives down and away from a batter (from a right-handed batter if you are right-handed, from a left-handed batter if you are left-handed.) You can often pitch a good game of ball even before you have learned to control the curve, if you can use it for a "waste" pitch, out of the strike zone, to make it harder for the batter to time your fast ball. But you should work hard to control the curve, to learn how to release it so that it will come into the strike zone when you want it to.

The philosophy of pitching and the art of pitching taught to me by some of the greatest pitching coaches in the history of the game included Charlie Dressen who brought Sandy Koufax and Don Drysdale into major league baseball and Johnny Sain, who pitched as a superstar and then was able to give that advice to others to master their trade.
There is a master theme to pitching and I am going to tell you what it is now.

Start by throwing fastballs to your hitters in the lineup. If two guys get hits off your fastball back to back then you can start throwing other pitches because it may mean that you either don't have a good fastball, or maybe that day you did not have a good fastball or you are just having a crazy bad day but you still can't give it up. I was taught until they hit two balls hard you don't have to worry about change in your plan of attack. The changeup should only be thrown when the count is even or your behind. Why would you throw a changeup when you have a guy no balls and two strikes? Why throw a change-up when you have the hitter deep in the hole? It does not make any sense and should never be done.

When you throw a changeup and you have two strikes on a hitter you are giving that guy a chance to put the ball in play. Remember when you've got a guy deep in the hole why give him something that is so slow and allows him to react and adjust with at least another half a second to adjust to the pitch and possibly hit a home run or something less. Remember no hitter has ever hit 1000 and only one great hitter, may be the greatest hitter of all time, Ted Williams, in the modern baseball era hit more than 400. There will never be another Ted Williams no matter how many home runs they hit.

Until you can do this you are not a complete pitcher. But do not get the idea that your job is to learn a lot of trick pitches. The name of the game is first-strikes-and then the position of those pitches. Another important fact for you as you learn the art of pitching:

Your test should be the following: If you at your age level are unable to get your age level hitters out, in other words kids that are in your age range with just the fastball, then either you must work harder, work with weights or concentrate on a another position and really concentrate on school and college. This does not mean that you cannot get a ride to school on a scholarship. If you are a very good player in high school colleges are going to offer you an opportunity to play for them. And of course in the college ranks, coaching, and the application of coaching get somewhat better.

My example for getting hitters out at your age: let's use the age of 14. If the players you are playing against are 13,14 or 15, you should always be able to get out at least 90% of those hitters with only your fastball.

When I was a major league pitcher for more than 10 years, I used to throw 85 to 90% fastballs. The key to my success was control. It was not the number of pitches that I threw. It was not the number of sliders, I threw, it was not the number of curveballs I threw or changeups. It was the number of times that I threw strikes or strikes that were close enough that hitters could not lay off the pitch. So our first lesson in this chapter is throw 90% fastballs, at least, to all hitters and if you get 90% of them out you have something very special.

Many young fellows fail to develop as pitchers because they spend so much time working on trick pitches- often pitches that require only part of his strength. As a result his arm never becomes as strong as it should and his number one weapon-the good fast ball- never picks up the speed it might have had.

And speaking of arms and the strength of arms. If you are only going to mess around sliders, curveballs, fork balls or other funny pitches that do not develop strength, but in a sense you are trying to get hitters out with "tricked pitches" then you are on the wrong course. No one ever got to the big leagues, at least no one I knew, without at least a good or better fastball.

Trying to develop junk pitches, tricked pitches and other garbage is surely a waste of time for all of us. Junk pitches should be developed after you have pitched a long time and at some point in time you realized that your fastball was not effective enough to get most hitters out so you give up the idea of professional baseball. But don't give up the idea for college. College has lower standards for people who can pitch and get hitters out, the bar is much lower. Always keep in mind, whatever the percentages but it sure seems like one in 10 million, ever gets to the major leagues and that can probably be said for all sports.

Now you will work on new pitches but first and again I say this you better have a good fastball.

In this book we will show you the grips and positions for some of these tricked pitches and as I call it junk.

Yes, everyone needs some off pitches but you don't need them until it's time and again you must make sure the instructor that is showing you the pitching techniques and the pitches knows what they are talking about. Nothing can be more harmful and dangerous to a young pitcher then learning the wrong way. I will repeat myself: nothing can be more harmful and dangerous to a young pitcher then learning the wrong way. At the age of 10,11 12,13 14,15 up to 18 you just don't have the strength to command these pitches.

Yes, you are going to need to have extra pitches eventually. But put them off until you have mastered the basic weapons, the fast ball and curve. Your arm grows strong from being used, at its full strength.

When you no longer can get hitters out with 90% fastballs, then it's time to look at other pitches and then it's time to consider once again your education and what you want to do the rest of your life.

My father once told me at the age of 13 that if he caught me throwing a curveball, because I had real good velocity at the age of 13, that he would break my arm for me. He did not want me to waste my arm since I threw the ball so hard by throwing junk. Junk that I could not throw because my arm was not strong enough to withstand the tension and pressure. About a year after my dad told me about breaking my arm if he caught me throwing a curveball, my dad passed away. He was my mentor, my teacher, he was my guy that I learned everything about baseball. Well after he died I decided that I don't know if he knew what he was talking about. I threw the ball hard why couldn't I throw a curveball. So I started experimenting with a curveball at the age of 13 1/2. Within two weeks of screwing around with the curveball I almost destroyed a possible major league career. I did not play the game of baseball because I hurt my arm so badly screwing around with a curveball and I did not throw for more than 3 to 4 months before I had the ability to throw the ball hard again and play the great game. Let that be a lesson, and no one knew the game and knew his son better than my dad and he knew that that curveball or that slider could cause great damage.

Let's talk about making your fastball better.
There are ways in order to build up your strength. Good fastballs. Well, a lot of people say pitchers are born the day you arrive in this world and that may be true, but there are ways if you have some decent velocity to improve your velocity at certain ages by 3 to 6 or 7 mph. I'm going to tell you now exercises that work and that have personally worked for me.
One: I used to lift 5 pound weights, only about 25 per day per arm focusing on my hand to my elbow. I did not turn or twist or try to do anything with my elbow or shoulder, except lift the 5 pound weight. In fact I would put my elbow on the table and lift 25 5 pound weights in a row and that would complete that

exercise. It is not a race. You should count them on a 1001 basis. In other words, every time you lift one you say 1001, then you say 1002, etc. This is not a race. This is a development of an individual who is trying to improve his fastball.

Two: I found bowling to be the most and best exercise that I ever had in my entire career. Now don't laugh and let me point out why bowling is so good. Every part of your body is being exercise when you bowl. Your feet, calves, knees, back muscles, your core, arms, forearms, shoulders, neck, and of course your head because you have a lot of thinking to do to make all of these different parts work at the same time. Bowling develops great rhythm and any time someone has great rhythm and great balance they normally are a pretty good athlete in some sport.

Three: running is a great exercise for all pitchers. Now, today, they have a different philosophy about running, they run less, but they also pitch less, go figure. I know that we were completing up to 20 games per year, and some of us more, and there was a reason for that. We did a lot of running in the outfield before and after a game. Running is one of the greatest exercises for all sports that one can ever use.

Four: lifting heavy weights. As far as I'm concerned, lifting heavy weights is a waste of time, unless you have a particular injury and you are trying to strengthen that injured area or part or arm or leg where you definitely need additional strength in a rehab environment. But I am not a fan of lifting 300 or 400 pounds. Pitchers do not need to be tight and built like a brick mortar house. The more flexible pitchers are, the more loose their muscles are, the better the pitcher will be. Remember, if you're going to pump iron every day do you want to look like the Hulk? Can you imagine what the Hulk would've suffered had he tried to pitch? Lifting hundreds of pounds in weight doesn't work unless you want to be a weightlifter, football player, possibly a hockey player, but not baseball. You don't need to lift huge weights. It's silly and it can be dangerous. Lifting heavy weights will also expose you to core muscle issues and you want to stay away from core muscle injuries and you don't want to do anything to put yourself in a position that you can injure your core.

Now let's position your fastball. We have a set of pictures in the book that shows you how and what will happen when you position your fingers and your hand in various positions on the baseball. All pictures have full explanations as to what the ball should do or should have a tendency to do. If you are holding the ball properly with the right amount of pressure. People don't realize there are so many things to think about when you throw pitches. And we will get into that later on in this book.

The fast ball is held in the finger tips- the two first fingers in top of the ball and the thumb underneath it. You hold the ball in a good tight grip. Unless you can grip the ball tightly you are not going to get the spin that makes the ball alive and gives it its jump. A strong grip is important to a pitcher. You would do well to exercise your grip at every chance. Squeezing a rubber ball that you carry around with you will provide extra exercise.

The curve, instead of being released off the tip of the fingers, like the fast ball, is released from the crotch between your forefinger and thumb, so the spin is provided by the edge of your finger rather than the tip. To release the ball this way, you will find that you must turn your hand over, and when you finish your pitch your hand will be upward. As you get used to throwing this pitch you will find that you can turn your hand over with extra snap to get more spin on this pitch. It is this spin that provides the "break"- the downward and outward movement that takes the ball away from the batter.

There are far more to these pitches than the way you hold and release them however. Your legs and your back have a great deal to do with the speed and effectiveness of your pitches. A windup is not too important; except that it helps you get all your muscles working in unison and may help in some ways to throw the batter off balance. What is important is getting your weight *behind* each pitch and changing your stride to suit the pitch. The pitcher starts his motion with his weight mostly on his pivot foot-that is, the foot on the same side as the throwing hand: Right foot for a right-handed pitcher; left foot for a left handed pitcher, the pitcher then reaches back, lifting his other foot and strides forward as he brings his arm down to complete the pitch.

The most common fault I have noticed in young pitchers is "pitching too quickly". That does not mean throwing too hard, or not waiting long enough between pitches. It means not taking the time to reach back to get your arm fully extended and your weight behind the rubber. Even in the big leagues you will see pitchers who never do lean back at all but pitch entirely from in front of the rubber. They can get by with this for a while if they are strong. But they will never get their full strength into their pitches this way and so will not be as effective as they could be. They are throwing almost entirely with their arms and not with their whole bodies.

The forward stride is made quickly, with a good shove off the rubber by the pivot foot. But do not make it too long. Make sure you come down on your toe, or with your knees bent, so you will be able to keep your balance. Bring your hind foot up quickly and face the batter with your knees bent and ready to move in any direction to field the ball.

The stride you take with the curve ball will be a little shorter than the one you use with the fast ball. A shorter stride gives you more chance to "pull down" on your curve. That is, it enables you to reach up a bit higher and bring your hand down further to provide extra time for that big turn of the wrist that puts the spin on the curve. A shorter stride of course means a little less beef behind your pitch, so the curve will not approach the batter with quite the speed of the fast ball. This in itself will provide a change of pace that will make it difficult for the batter to time your pitches. Some pitchers get along for some time with only the curve for a change of pace.

Some pitchers like to throw the curve sidearm. Finding it easier, with the sidearm motion, to release the ball in the proper way. In fact it is more natural, in this motion, to release the ball off the side of the hand. But I think it is wrong to use a different motion for your curve. To the batter, the curve should look just like a fast ball until it is well on its way. If he can see the curve coming in advance, he can get ready for it and is far more likely to hit it safely. But if you throw both fast ball and curve with either the full overhand or three-quarters overhand motion, you will not permit the batter to anticipate the pitch.

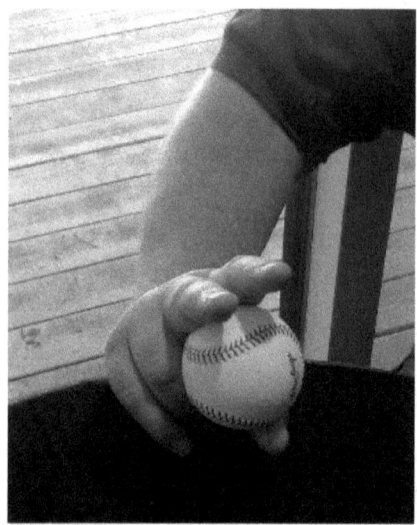

Change up

The curve, because of the need for releasing it off the sides of finger and thumb, must be held somewhat deeper in the hand than the fast ball. You must be careful however not to let the batter see you adjusting the ball in your hand. And above all you must take care not to make the mistake some pitchers sometimes make-that is, looking down at the ball to make sure it is well placed in your hand. That is a sure tip-off that the curve is coming. You must also watch out that you do not limit your wind-up on the curve, as you may be tempted to do. If you raise both hands right up over your head when you start your fast ball motion, be sure you do exactly the same thing for your curve ball motion.

When you have got both fast ball and curve working- when you can put either one into the strike zone when you want to- then it will be time enough to start practicing that extra pitch. The best one of course is a real change up- a pitch that shows dramatic change in speed from your regular pitches. I think the easiest change-up is the ball that is thrown with the fingertips lifted off the ball as you release it. If you grip the ball, not with the tips of your fingers but with the first joints, you will find it fairly easy to lift your finger tips as you release the ball. The ball, when thrown this way, will have very little spin and so will not be nearly so fast as it is when you throw it out of a tight grip. The manner in which you deliver the ball should in every other way, *look* just like a fast-ball delivery. But it cannot be *exactly* like it or you will not get the sharp change in speed that you are after. In practicing this pitch, you should take care not to shove off the rubber too hard with your pivot foot. As a matter of fact, I think the best way to learn control this pitch is to throw it for a while without pulling your foot up as you deliver it. Leaving your hind foot on the rubber or dragging it up very *slowly* will help you make a habit of not putting to much strength in this pitch. As you get the pitch under control, so that you can put it into the strike zone whenever you want to, you can begin to complete your motion by bringing that hind foot up- not with a shove but with a lift and a step- so that your motion is complete.

You will see some strong pitchers who depend on a full long stride to get fire into their fast ball. A long stride means coming down on your heel, or with a stiff leg, so that your spine is jarred momentarily and your vision is blurred. Or it may mean stumbling off balance and actually falling down. The way to compensate for a long stride- if you *must* take one- is to start with your knees bent. Having your body in a sort of "Coiled spring" position like this enables you to get your throw off fast.

You want to get your throw off especially fast when you have men on base. If it takes you extra time to get cranked up to throw, the runner is going to have that extra time to cover the distance between bases.

The Art Of Pitching

Completing the pitching delivery, land with the knees bent and feet parallel, ready to field the ball if it comes back to you.

You will need to put in some hard practice in pitching from the "stretch" position, which is what you will use with runners on base. In this position, you stand in front of the rubber, with your pivot foot in contact. As you start your delivery, your weight will be almost entirely on your pivot foot. Then you lift your other foot and take a quick stride toward the plate. But you must not shorten your arm as you throw. You still must *reach* back and throw with the full length of your arm. Do not try to pitch by just cocking the arm and snapping off the throw. That will not only rob you of most of your power but it will eventually spoil your arm.

With men on base, you have to take charge. Don't let them intimidate you. Instead, *you* intimidate them. Be aggressive. Don't hesitate to throw to the base when they seem to be taking too long a lead, or when they are "leaning" the wrong way- that is, putting their weight on the foot nearest the other base.

The rule keeps you from faking a man back to first base by pretending to throw there. They also prevent you from taking you position in the rubber (or near it) without the ball in your possession. So you must practice keeping the runner from reading your move. Practice keeping all your movements the same until the time you actually step forward to release the ball. For the throw to the plate and the throw to the base, lift your front foot and cock your leg in *exactly* the same way. Reach back to throw just as you reach back to pitch.

But *never* change your mind in the middle of your motion. If you are going to the plate, you must decide to do so from the start of your motion. But you must keep the runner from figuring out what your decision is.

Runners have different ways of stealing. Some of them like to take a generous lead, then perform a few dancing steps or fake starts to keep the pitcher off balance. Some of them will actually walk off the base and keep right on walking, never stopping unless the pitcher is obviously ready to shoot them down. Some of them will take all the lead you will allow them and poise there in their toes, ready to explode into a run as soon as you start to go to the plate. But remember, if your motion is well-practiced, they can't know for sure exactly when your throw is going to the plate, so they are going to have to guess- to take a chance on getting the jump. Often you can outguess them.

To keep track of the runner, you don't have to turn away from the plate. You don't have to see the runner's whole body or read the expression on his face. You just have to see his feet. If a runner had a standard lead- the length of his body plus one stride, he can usually get back with a dive even if he does not see the throw coming until you are ready to release it. But if he takes any more than that, and seems to have his weight leaning toward the next base, then you have a good chance of nailing him. Don't be afraid to throw hard.

If the runner is one of those who walk away from the base, you can probably stop him just by staring him down. Look right at him, with the ball in your hand, until he stops. In order to stop a runner, or keep him from getting too frisky with his lead, you may have to lift your pivot foot and set it behind the rubber. This sets you free from the rule that keeps you from breaking your motion. And it enables you to move right back toward the baseline if the runner does not get back. (When your foot is on the rubber, you are obliged to throw in the direction of your step.) If a guy keeps edging up the baseline, even when you step back off the rubber, then you should move straight toward him with the ball in your hand and drive him one way or the other. You have charge of the baseball so you can throw to the base as often as you like. If a man keeps on taking too big a lead, or persists in moving up the baseline, keep trying to catch him. When you finally have his lead cut down, or has him leaning back to his own base, then give up on him and make up your mind to throw to the plate. Don't let him know your decision, but don't let him change your mind when you have started your motion. Just forget about him and concentrate on pitching to the batter.

Left handed pitchers have the edge on right hander's because they are facing the runner on first. But if you are left handed, don't let it make you careless about developing that move toward the base. Study at it and get your team mates to watch it until you are sure they can't too quickly detect the difference between throw and pitch. You should be able to get your motion well started- your front foot lifted your arm back- before there is any detectable difference between the throw to the plate and the throw to the base.

When you have a runner at second base who is taking a lead, you do not have quite such a tough problem as when he is on first. You can step toward him without throwing. You can even pretend to throw in order to get him back to the base. But to pick off a runner on second base, you need to have a pick-off play worked out with your catcher and second baseman. When you have practiced such a play, you do not need to keep watching the runner. The catcher will do that for you. He will give a signal, meaning the play is on and the second baseman is starting for the bag. Practice will have shown you how long it takes the second baseman to get to the bag and you can begin to count to yourself. When you reach the agreed count, you turn and quickly fire the ball hard- not at the bag but at a spot just on the fielder's side of the bag, so he will get the ball in stride before he reaches the base. You want him to have the ball in his glove when he gets there.

There is one runner you must never forget about. He is the runner on third. When you have a man on third who may steal home, always be sure to take a look at him before you go into your pitch. Otherwise he may take off before you go into your motion and be halfway home before you even know he has started. Take a good long look at such a runner. Make sure he has cut down on his lead, or has started back to third, before you start to work on the batter. It is usually easy to stare down this runner. Just keep your eyes on him, no matter how he bluffs and fakes, until he had moved back toward the bag. If he persists in hanging on to a dangerous lead-if he gets farther away from the base than the fielder is- make a try to pick him off. And don't *ever, ever* forget to look at him.

As a matter of fact, when you have runners on base, you must be sure to look at them all. You don't have to hustle your pitch. Check the runners carefully. Be sure they are not holding an oversize lead and are not moving toward the next base. Step off the rubber, if need be, to quiet them down. Only then can you put them out of your mind and *pitch*.

Chapter 2

Sizing up The Batters

When you face a batter for the first time, you cannot really tell by looking at him what sort of hitter he is or what sort of pitch is likely to get him out. But you can be sure of one thing: the chances are very good that he cannot hit a *low* pitch very far. Once in a while you run into a batter who can golf a low pitch out of the park. But believe me he is a rarity. A low pitch is hard to hit anyway, because a batter does not see quite so much of the ball, for quite so long. A high pitch can be seen full size all the way to the plate. But before a low pitch gets to the plate, the batter is looking down on it and so cannot see quite so much ball. Consequently he is not so likely to hit it squarely. And if he does hit a low pitch the ball is very likely to be a ground ball that can be fielded before it gets out of the infield. So it is to your advantage to keep the ball below the batter's waist.

A high pitch of course can be useful, when you want to put a pitch out of the strike zone, where the batter, if he hits the ball, cannot hit it with much power. Or it can be handy to help keep the batter off balance and unsure of where the next pitch is coming.

But we are talking about a batter you have never faced before. You decide to keep the ball low, in the strike zone, to get ahead of him right away if you can. But what else?

The hitter

If he is a big strong looking fellow who swings the full length of the bat, the chances are he likes an outside pitch, fairly high. So you give him an outside pitch low, or you give him his pitch so close to him that he can do nothing with it. In other words, you try to make him hit *your* pitch, offering him something he is likely to swing at but not that you know or think he wants.

The fellows who crowd the plate are usually men who prefer an inside pitch. They stand close to the plate so that you are going to have to give them "their" pitch in the strike zone. So you give them a pitch that is down and away. Or if you come inside, you come in above the strike zone, where they will give you either a foul or a pop-up.

Just studying the position a batter takes will not, of course, provide you with the answer to what he wants to hit. Some batters, especially in the big leagues, will fool you completely by their stances. Some fellows will stand so far from the plate you would never believe they could even reach an outside pitch, let alone hit it safely. And then they'll step right into the pitch and knock it from here to there.

But when you are trying to figure out a strange batter it helps to go by a few general rules. After you have seen a batter a few times you should be able to remember what you got him out with or what he hit best.

A man who stands up forward in the box can do a better job on the curve. And the man who stands far back probably prefers the fast ball. So you take care, for starters, not to give them the kind of ball they seem able to hit best-or don't give it to them where they can do any damage with it.

In your contest with the hitter, you are trying to get him into a position where he will have no choice but to swing at the pitch you can get him out on. That means that you need to get the count in your favor as quickly as possible. There was a time years ago, when baseball was very different, and when the strike zone was much bigger than they have made it today, when batters almost always laid off the first pitch and so pitchers would use their second best at first. But now if you give a batter a weak pitch for the start, he is going to cream it. You have to get that first pitch into the strike zone with plenty of mustard on it, if you want to get a jump on the batter. Once you have the count in your favor, you can begin to work on him, trying to set him up for the pitch you plan to get him out on. So you must know what your strongest pitch is…that is the pitch you have best control of. Let that be your first pitch and give it all you've got.

But don't let anything I have said make you believe that the only thing that matters is an ability to control the ball. Of course without control, you can't be a pitcher. But if you let yourself get control happy, you may be only half a pitcher. There have been a number of very talented pitchers in the leagues who let their real talents go to waste because they concentrated too much on trying to achieve pin-point control. When you do that-when you try to place the ball into some precise spot in the strike zone, you are not going to be throwing it with your full strength. You may think you are pouring it in hard, but you won't be because you'll be concentrating too much on your aim. You must tell yourself over and over again one important fact: If you get the ball over the plate with zip on it, it is going to act alive—that is, it is going to be clipping the corners of the strike zone.

You do have to change your pattern too, as well as keeping the ball alive. If you get into a rut with your pitches-first high inside then low outside-or if you have only one good pitch and use that all the time, the batters will soon have you sized up and will be getting you in the hole rather than vice versa. So even if your curve ball is not too good and you don't have complete control of it, throw it now and then-especially if you are ahead of the batter. Use it as a "waste" pitch, one that does not need to come into the strike zone. Then the batter will not be quite so certain of what to expect. Take care, too, to keep changing the sequence of your pitches and move the ball, throwing into all different parts of the strike zone.

Basically, you are trying to keep the batter off balance by not letting him time your pitches or anticipate where the ball will be thrown. Of course a really fiery fast ball upsets any man's timing because it just comes down too fast for anyone to get set for it. But changes in the pitching motion and changes in the speed with which the ball is thrown as well as changes in the spot thrown to will keep a batter wondering, too. That is why it is well not to let yourself get in to a routine of any sort while pitching. You must keep changing the order of your pitches and keep putting them into different slots in and around the strike zone. Often an elaborate wind-up, with a head-fake in it, or an especially big kick, or an occasional shift in the extent of the wind-up (hand coming just over the head rather than behind it) will compensate for a lack of blinding speed or a sharp curve.

In spite of yourself, you are going to get behind in the count to the hitter from time to time, and you will be forced to give him a good pitch to keep him from getting in too deep a hole. In such moments, a real sharp change up is useful, for it will enable you to give the batter a pitch about the place he wants it, yet offer it with so much less than your normal speed that he may be off balance when he hits it and so unable to get his full strength into the swing. Heavy hitters are often easily tempted by these fat looking pitches that do not get to the plate quite as soon as the batter expects them.

It is not a good strategy however to use slow pitches on weak batter. Such men usually shorten up on the bat a little and slap the ball into spots. They are more adept at timing a pitch. And sometimes an off-speed pitch is about the only kind of pitch they can hit well. The weak batters in a line-up are the men who are going to provide you most of your outs. The heavy hitters are going to get their hits anyway and you sometimes can only give thanks that they did not hit the ball far, or did not hit it with runners on base. Of course you must work hard on the weak hitters, too. Use your best stuff on the lower end of the batting order. Get them out of there fast and don't let them put runs on base to be waiting there when the tough hitters come up.

The catcher.

Your catcher is the man who can help you most in sizing up batters. He is closer to them and ordinarily he will see them more often. You should always discuss with your catcher how you are going to deal with the batters you are about to face. Take his advice, if you can. You do not always have to throw the pitch he asks for, but if he insists on a certain pitch, even after you have shaken off his sign, go talk to him. Maybe he noticed something about the batter that has escaped you. Maybe the batter has moved a step closer to the plate, so that a different type of pitch will be more effective. Maybe he has edged up in the box, looking for the curve. The catcher is not going to make you throw any pitch you don't want to throw. But if he has some good reason for his call, you want to find out what it is.

Whatever happens, do not let the batters intimidate you and don't let them set the pace of the game. A good many young pitchers, in my observation, seem afraid to put a ball in the strike zone when there is a heavy hitter facing them. There are times, naturally, when it is good to "pitch around" a strong hitter to keep him from hitting the ball solidly-when you can afford to take a chance walking him rather than risk his breaking up the ballgame. But, except for these instances, you should be ready to challenge every batter, no m9atter what his record or reputation may be. Don't be timid about slamming that ball into the strike zone with plenty of zip. Tell yourself he just *can't* hit your good pitch.

Batters generally prefer to have a pitcher work fast. They come up to the plate eager to hit and are glad to have the ball offered up to them without delay. But you should make them wait a little, especially if there are men on base. I don't mean that you should stall, because the umpire won't allow that. But if you have the ball and they are going to have to wait for you before the game can get going. Check the base runners. Be satisfied with the sign. Make sure you are properly placed on the runner and that you can get a good grip on the ball. Take a good deep breath and settle yourself down. If you feel yourself getting tenses up or nervous, call your catcher out and talk things over for a few seconds.

Chapter 3

That Extra Pitch

When you have a fast ball, curve, and change-of-pace under control, so that you can get any one of them into the strike zone when you have to, it will be time enough to start work on one of those "extra" pitches that young fellows sometimes seem eager to learn.

A professional pitcher usually needs an extra pitch, to serve him when the going gets tough and the batters have begun to time his best stuff. But don't start to work on extra pitches-particularly pitch that do not require the full strength of your arm- before you have got your growth and developed your full strength. It troubles me to see youngsters in high school age or younger working, for instance, on a knuckle ball. No doubt about it, a knuckle ball is a fine pitch to have if you can control it. But spending time on it before your arm is at full strength will rob you of a chance to develop the pitching muscles. And a strong are that can deliver a sizzling fast ball or a curve that "drops off the table" is far more important to a young pitcher than a knuckle ball. This pitch and the other "extras"- the slider, the sinker, and the screwball- can all be developed as you go along and *after* you have the basic pitches in your repertoire.

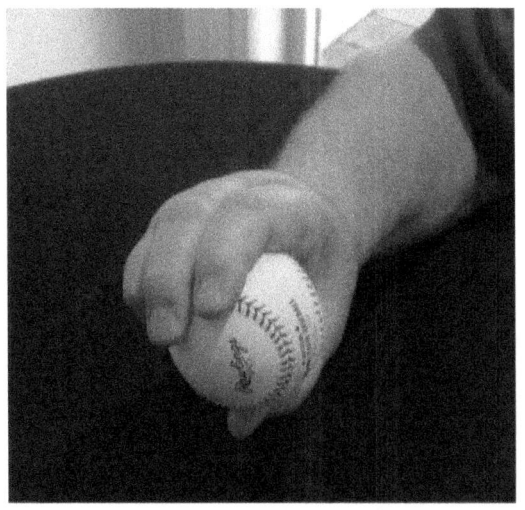

Slider

The slider, or the nickel curve, is a sort of fast-ball curve, thrown like a fast ball except that the hand is "cut away" from the ball as you release it, pretty much as you would throw a football. You do not turn your hand completely over, so you do not get the spin that a curve requires. But you do get spin enough to move the ball our of a straight path, so the ball comes up like a fast ball and acts enough like a curve to make a batter's life miserable. In gripping the ball for this pitch, it is best to put most of the pressure on with your middle finger. Throw hard but instead of taking the arm all the way through, as you do on a fast ball, cut the hand away and bring it down across your body. You will have to practice and practice to perfect this pitch but you can get some y of your practicing done during ball games, when you have a chance to waste a pitch or two.

Sinker

One of the hardest pitches for a batter to handle is the sinker. When a good sinker-ball pitcher is working, you will seldom see a ball hit into the air and almost never see one hit for distance. The sinker is almost the opposite of the slider. It too is thrown like a fast ball except that, as the ball is delivered, the hand is cut away with a *reverse* turn. That is, the hand is turned in the direction of the thumb, with the ball rolling off the inside of the fingers. There is no wrist-snap in this delivery. You simply turn the hand at the completion of the motion. This causes the ball to break down and in on the batter (provided he is a right hander and you are a right hander) and throws him off just as the slider does.

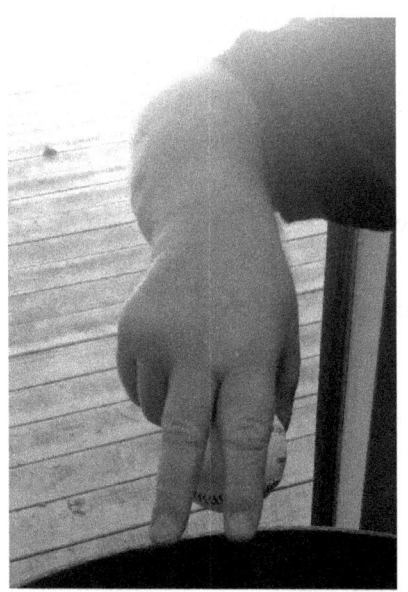

In throwing the sinker, the gripping of the ball is done mostly with the *index* finger and thumb. This makes it move in the direction opposite from the slider and gives it enough of a downward spin to cause it to drop rather suddenly when it reaches the plate. Also the sinker is most effective if you do not fire it with all your strength, but treat it rather like a change up. This means that in practicing this pitch, you should start by leaving your foot on the rubber to complete the motion and only gradually practice moving the pivot foot up, *without any shove*, to bring it alongside the other foot and leave you facing the batter. You can't be in a hurry about developing this pitch because it is going to take you some time to get to you can control it, and lift your hind foot off the rubber so that the delivery *looks* like a fast ball.

A screw ball is thrown pretty much like a sinker with one big difference: The hand is turned right over in the "reverse" direction, with a strong snap f your wrist, as on a curve, except that you turn your hand the other way, winding up with the palm of your hand turned toward the batter. This pitch too is distinctly slower than a good fast ball and serves some men as a change of pace. Thrown low and on the outside, it can be a real killer, for it will look as if it is going to miss the plate by inches, then will break in and pick up the corner.

The knuckle ball is held in the fingertips with the hand behind the ball. This gets the ball off without any spin.

The Art Of Pitching

The knuckle ball is no longer thrown from the knuckles. Pitchers have found it works best as a finger-tip ball. To throw it well you are going to have to keep your nails will manicure. You may use it with two finger-tips gripping the ball on top. Well, I should not say on top, because actually the hand is held *behind* the ball in this pitch and the throw is a sort of push off the fingers, rather than with a spin.

Because the thumb provides most of the friction, this serves to counteract the normal spin of the ball and as a result there is practically no spin at all-just a sort of wobbling weave, with the seams visible as the ball flies toward the batter. It is this odd appearance of the ball-seeming to float along on a weaving path-that provides the "flutter" that has earned the pitch the name of the butterfly ball. Actually it does not really flutter. It just looks so startlingly close, with the seams all visible, that it looks as if it is on top of you when it still has some distance to go. Both the catcher and batter are fooled by this illusion and you will often see the catcher scrambling into the dirt to get hold of the ball he thought was coming straight into his mitt.

The knuckleball, like every other off speed pitch, including the sinker, requires extra practice to avoid shoving off the rubber with the pivot foot. You will have to throw it for a while, with the pivot foot allowed to stay on the rubber and, only when you have it well under control, begin lifting the pivot foot and bring it up to plant it along side the front foot. Of course you won't use the knuckleball in a game until you are able to deliver it with a good approximation of your regular motion and stride. If you take my advice, you won't even think about it, or practice it at all, until you have got your full arm strength and growth.

In general then, your development as a pitcher should be like this: First the fast ball, with up and down control. Then the side-to-side control of the fast ball. Then the curve, using it sparingly as a sort of change-of-pace, until you have it under control. You'll go a long way with these two pitches. Next, you will add a change up of some sort. I recommend the straight change (thrown of the fast ball motion) rather than the curve ball change because the result is more unexpected from the batter's view. Only after you have all these pitches working for you, and working well, so you can put then into the strike zone anytime you like, should you work on the "extra" pitches. They can be practiced in your spare time and gradually introduced into the regular competition- first as waste pitches and finally as a regular part of your equipment.

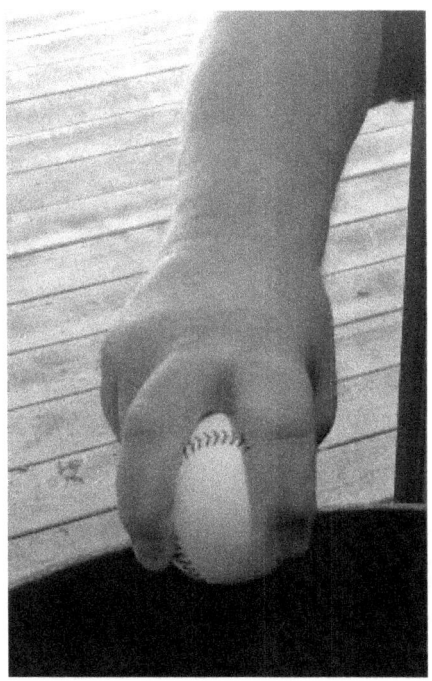

Forkball

Chapter 4

Playing a Ball Game

A pitcher should never forget that he is a baseball player- a member of a team. He must be ready to field baseballs that are hit back within his reach and he must be ready to cover bases and back up throws. Train yourself therefore to get into fielding position after every pitch. You should be facing the batter, after the pitch had been delivered. Your feet should be side by side. Your weight should be on the balls of your feet. Your back and your knees should be bent. Your hands should be out in front of you. You should be ready to move in any direction. Don't think that, because the ball is not often hit to you, it never will be. And don't tell yourself that it probably won't be this time. You must expect *every* pitch to come back to you. Be ready.

If the ball is bunted within your reach, you are going to have to field it and throw it to base. Sacrifice bunts are always telegraphed by the batter, who will turn around and face you directly, with the bat in bunting position. When you know a bunt is coming, follow your pitch by taking two quick steps toward the batter. Then be ready to move to whatever side the ball is bunted on. Don't panic or try to throw too quickly. Keep your eye on the ball! Most bunted balls that are mishandled are booted because the fielder tries to pick up the ball while he is looking at the base. Never mind how easy it looks to do this. Watch that ball right into your glove. And don't be fancy with it. Always use two hands in fielding. Round the ball up with your glove and take hold of it in your bare hand. Then, when you *see* the ball in your hand, turn and look at your target.

Sometimes, if the ball is fielded quickly, there may be a chance to spoil the sacrifice by nailing the lead runner. Your catcher or another fielder will let you know about that. But as you get ready to throw, no matter how many team mates are shouting "Second base!" as you are ready to throw, you have to make sure that second based is covered. Do not throw blindly to the base. Look to see that someone is there to take the throw. Then fire it there *hard*, about chest high. If you don't see a fielder there, don't wait for him. The batter is now racing down the baseline toward first. Better get him out than lose both men, so fire to first base, *inside* the baseline.

Pop flies are best left to the fielders who have practiced in catching them, or to the catcher. Even if the ball is popped right over the pitchers mound, it is better to get right out of there and allow an infielder to handle it. He will be moving toward the ball, will have a better angle on it and will have a longer look at it. You might back up and stumble over the rubber.

But you should always "Captain" a pop fly near the plate by calling out to the catcher whether he or one of the basemen should catch the ball. Do not let two fielders collide under such a fly. If they do not pay attention to your call, then run right over and grab one of them to keep him from crashing into the other guy. A collision with a catcher can put a fielder out of the game.

On unexpected bunts or squeeze bunts or baseline bunts that are hard to get to, the same advice applies as on simple sacrifice: Keep your eye on the ball until you have it safely in your hand. *Then* look at your target and throw to a fielder. Once in a while, with a bunt on the third base line, you are going to have to ignore the field-with-both-hands advice and try to scoop it and get the throw off in almost the same motion. But here it is even more important that you first keep your eye on the ball until you have it in your hand and then see your target before you throw.

When a ball is hit to your left, it may be necessary for the first baseman to field it. This means that you will have to cover first to make the out. So school yourself, *every* time a ball is hit to your left to start moving toward first. Sometimes the ball will be yours to field and you should try to field it with both hands. But if you miss it, do not chase after it. Keep right on going for first. There may still be time to nail the runner if the first baseman fields the ball. But you must be there to get the throw.

On a play at first, because you will be moving directly across the path of the runner, you should change direction as you cross the bag. Turn and run a course parallel to the runner's, so you will not crash into him or get yourself spiked.

The base you will have to backup most frequently is third base. Whenever you see a possible play developing that will bring a throw from the outfield to third base, hustle over there and prepare to field an overthrow. That does not mean that you should stand and look over the third-baseman's shoulder. You have got to get far enough behind him so that a bad throw will not miss you both. Twenty five to thirty feet is the proper distance.

Denny McLain

You should also take care never to leave home plate uncovered. If the catcher, when there are runners on base, has to go back to the screen for a foul ball, remember that if there are less than two outs a runner can advance after the catch. You should get down to the plate, if there is a runner on third, and prepare to take a throw. If a runner may advance from first, the shortstop will probably come to the mound to act as relay on the throw. But if he forgets then you remember. On possible throws to the catcher from the outfield, say with a man on second and the ball is hit to center or left, your best spot is part way down the baseline between third and home-about two thirds of the way down. Here you can back up the throw to the third baseman and also be ready to back up the catcher if the throw comes to him-or cover the plate if he is pulled away.

On any ball hit to the outfield the pitcher should turn and size up the developing play. If there is likely to be a throw, then the pitcher should get into the spot where he can be the most help. He should never try to act as the "cut-off" man, because that is a job for an experienced infielder. But he should place himself where he can retrieve an overthrow, or cover a vacated base. When the catcher has to chase a runner back toward third base, the pitcher should get in and cover the plate, and be ready to play a part in a possible rundown.

In short, do not let yourself be found anchored to the rubber while there is action all around you. Move into positions to help whenever you can. And practice fielding every chance you get. Work hard to develop the habit of breaking toward first base on *any* ball hit to your left. Many times, you'll not be needed. But it is better to be there ten times when you are not needed than to be missing when you are needed.

Pitching a baseball game is a whole lot different from merely pitching to the plate in practice. In a game, you have got to take command-of yourself and of the ball game. You have got to *concentrate*. And you have got to be ready to reach down into your reserve strength and use up the last ounce of your energy, even at the cost of some pain.

Concentration is the key

Taking command of yourself means controlling your temper, or at least keeping from making a show of it. There are a few sights more demoralizing to your team mates and more encouraging to the batter than a pitcher in a fit of temper. That is why some players make a special point of needling the pitcher- of shouting comments to him that they know will get under his skin. They know that when a man loses control of his temper he is very likely to lose control of the baseball too.

There will be times of course when you get so disgusted with yourself that you will feel like pounding yourself on the head. There will be times when you feel ready to pound the *umpire* on the head. And sometimes a stupid misplay that keeps you from getting out of a tight spot will make you mad enough to shoot. But *every time* something like that happens, fight to keep from showing your feelings. Take a deep breath. Take a look at the outfield, at the sky, at the fence. Talk to yourself silently. *Don't* give way.

Slamming your glove down, kicking up bits of dirt, screaming curses, throwing your hands in the air- all of that is kindergarten stuff. Often it is just an effort to show that *you* are not to blame. Burt whatever the motive, it is no help to either you or your team. One serious result of such antics is often the breaking of your own concentration.

Nowadays it seems to me that more and more athletes are beginning to realize the value of *concentration.* Sometimes I think it is concentration as much as talent that separates the winners from the losers. Concentration is certainly the mark of the real pro. Lack of concentration is what causes errors in baseball, fumbles, dropped passes, and missed tackles in football, and missed goals in basketball and soccer and many other disasters.

Concentration means taking the game seriously—and more than that, taking *every play* and *every pitch* seriously. When you are in school, you often need only that desperate urge to win to keep you concentrating. In professional sports you have pride and the desire o get ahead in your profession to motivate you. But whatever your goal may be, you are going to have to learn to concentrate your whole mind, heart, and energy on the job at hand. You cannot afford, when you are trying to win a ball game, to let your attention wander or to get half-hearted or to assume that you don't have to work too hard this time. There will be spots-when you have a fat lead and everybody on your side is hitting- when you may not need to bear down. I have even heard tell of a pitcher's feeding a fat pitch to Mickey Mantle once, when the game was not in danger. But you can *never* get careless. And you must treat every batter as a separate job and every pitch as a complete effort.

When you are ready to pitch to the man at the plate, you must put everything else out of your mind and put your whole heart into doing *exactly right* with the pitch you have planned. Decide just what you should throw, depending on the batter's skill, the count, and the game situation. Then put everything you've got into pitching exactly the sort of ball you intend to throw. If you give up a home run, even a grand slam home run, you cannot take the time to mope about it. There is a new batter coming to the plate, a new job to do that requires your full attention. You cannot afford to dwell on what just went wrong. Now you have to decide how you are going to deal with this batter. What does he like to hit? What can you get him out on? How will you set him up for that get-out pitch?

Sometimes you will find that your fast ball has lost some of its zip. Do not be stubborn about it. Recognize your limitations and use your next best pitch as your chief weapon, with your fast ball saved for use as a waste pitch or in spots where you can afford the risk. Often you will find that the fast ball comes back during a game and you can start to use it again. But never pitch yourself into a hole because you refuse to believe your stuff is not as good as ever. Nearly every pitcher hates to be taken out of a game and there are very few will admit out loud that they probably can't get the next man out. It is good to have that attitude. But don't fool yourself. If your best weapon had lost its edge, use the next best for a while.

When you are on the bench between innings, don't let your attention wander. Think about the men you will face next inning and plan how you are going to deal with each one. If there is some man coming up who has special habits or skills, go over them in your mind. If he is a hit and run man, talk about him to your catcher. If he is on a hot streak, think about using a different strategy on him. Just stay in the ball game all the time and always be ready to use your full strength when it is needed.

This willingness to use up the last bit of strength is what makes men into champions. If you work hard as a pitcher, you will often find yourself in a spot where you feel you have hardly any strength left-when you ache and feel almost ready to drop. The instinct then is to quit and go take a shower or to ease up on the pitches and just hope nothing happens to hurt you.

But suppose you have the bases full, with the tying run on second base. You are leading 2 to 0 in the last of the ninth. In a moment like that, you have to fight your instinct and reach down deep into your reserves strength, into the strength that non-athletes know nothing about. Into the reserve you have build through regular and even punishing exercise. You must dig in there and against the will of your body, force it to perform just a little longer with full strength-just long enough to get the last men out. It can be done. It has been done. No one ever won a championship without an effort of this sort.

In addition to concentration, when you are playing a real ball game, you must have confidence. You must *know* you can get the batters out. You must *know* you can pick that smart-alec base runner off first any time he takes too big a lead. You must *know* you can put good pitches into the strike zone. You build confidence of course by pitching successfully. But you also build it by practicing hard and developing your ability to the point where you *know* it is top-notch. After that, don't let anyone or anything shake your confidence. Don't let heavy hitters scare you or fast base runners upset you. Keep your cool at all times, even if you have to stop the ball game for a moment or two to get a good grip on yourself. Don't ever get to the point where you would prefer not to pitch to a certain batter. Your reaction to a home run or a fence-rattling hit should be an eagerness to get at the next batter and show him that the hit was pure luck. You should feel a real desire to get out to the mound and start daring those batters to hit your good stuff.

Be aggressive at all times. Do not fret about what some batter may be about to do to your best pitch. Instead plan what you are going to do to him. When you walk out to the mound at the start of the game, tell yourself, "This is *my* ball game!" Then look at every batter as if he were a guy come to take away something that belongs to you.

You do not of course carry this aggressiveness to a point where you use it blindly and try just to blow the ball past every batter. Be proud of your craft as well as your strength. When you have a big eager hitter at bat, with men on base and first base open, you do not need to put the ball in the strike zone at all. Just flirt with it. Tease him and make him start lunging at the ball if you can. Let him walk if need be. Just don't let up on him by giving him the pitch he is straining for. Sometimes you can even strike out one of these eager beavers by giving him the pitch right in the dirt.

When you have a good lead and your side is hitting well, you do not ease up. Instead you start throwing nothing but strikes-hard strikes, so that anybody who wants to get on base is going to have to hit the ball to get there.

Many times, when a batter is obviously planning to bunt it is better to let him bunt than to give him a free base just from trying to keep the ball away from him. But in a tight game it is sometimes important to try to make it difficult for a batter to bunt-as when a squeeze play seems in order, and the batter *must* bunt to protect the runner who starts for home with the pitch. The best ball to throw then is high and tight. It takes skilled batsmen to get such a pitch on the ground. It usually means a foul or a pop-up.

You should always remind yourself that there are fielders behind you and you should not ignore them as you pitch. Look around and see how they are placed and take advantage of their position. That is, if your fielders are set to keep a man from moving from second to third, you should cooperate by trying to pitch so that the batter will have a hard time hitting the ball to the right side of the diamond. Inside pitches to a right hander and outside pitches to a left hander will make it more likely that a ball that is hit will go to the left handed side, the batters that is.

If your fielders are playing in tight to cut off a run, you should cooperate by avoiding any high pitches that can be looped over their heads. Or if you want to pitch a certain way to some batter turn to make sure your fielders are placed so as to be ready for the type of hit your pitch is likely to produce. If you are not satisfied with their positions, ask them to shift.

Do not find fault with your fielders, no matter how badly they play ball up a play, or how tough the going is. They are your team mates the only ones you are likely to have for this game at least, and you have got to pull it all together. Put the error out of your mind. You may even want to take a second or two first to cheer up the man that made it and assure him you are going to get the next guy. Then put your mind on that next man and do your best to keep your promise.

In a hard fought game, you may start to tire and find that it is hard to control your good pitches. Your curve may be missing the strike zone, or it may not be breaking as it should. Then you may want to shorten your stride just a bit, to give you more "air" to snap off your curve in. Or you may want to shift your position on the rubber to make sure you hit the strike zone. If your fast ball starts coming in high, check your own motion. Make sure you are not "pitching straight up"-that is, without bending your back. And be sure you get your back into every pitch, even if you have to pace yourself a bit more slowly. Going wild high is a sign you are tiring and you must be sure you get plenty of oxygen (deep breaths!) and time between pitches to summon your strength.

Above all, don't give up on your good pitches. Don't start throwing trick pitches in tight spots. A hard fast ball is almost always the best weapon. But if your best pitch is your curve, don't abandon it because of weariness. The tougher the situation, the more important it is to go with your best.

Chapter 5

Exercise and Equipment

The very best exercise for a pitcher, except for throwing, is *running*. Run some every day (except the day you pitch. Cut down a little the day after you pitch. But every other day run, run, run.

Do not just take a warm up jog; punish yourself! Run about half an hour and run hard, until your muscles start to complain and the perspiration really pours. This is the way to build your stamina that will come to your rescue when fatigue seems about to knock you out. You should run in the winter time, too and try to keep in good shape, both muscles and wind, all year round.

Stay away from between meal snacks that put lard around your belt. Eat hearty, well balanced meals. Eat that you like. But don't go on eating binges or stuff yourself when you are not hungry. Find out what your best weight is and keep a check on it. When the scales go even a fraction over that weight- cut down on the intake!

The most important part of your equipment will be your glove. Make it a big one- as big as they allow. The pitcher needs it to knock down those hot shots that come right back at him. And he needs it for protection. It also helps in concealing the position of his hand and wrist and fingers and in concealing the ball.

Shoes are important too. Always have two pairs of shoes- one to work out in and one to pitch in. Never pitch a ball game in shoes that are loose or that have loose spikes. You want shoes that fit snugly with good sharp spikes, well fasten to the soles. A toe-plate is necessary too, to absorb the wear on your pivot shoe as you drag it over the rubber. But don't get one that will come lose. Leather is best.

For the rest, to succeed at pitching you need the FOUR C's:

Control, Condition, Concentration, and Confidence.

Now, get out there and pitch!

TALENT AND FAST BALLS

Since our great game of baseball began, the everyday coaches have tried to come up with a new wheel for training pitchers, almost every coach I have met in professional baseball and in some cases even high school base their methods on what they think not what has worked historically.

If coaches base their coaching on conventional principles, good things will happen but trying to invent the new wheel would only cause the young pitchers lots of issues including sore arms and possibly something even worse, surgical procedures. Fads and gimmicks don't work.

Remember the best way to professional baseball and college scholarships is an above average fastball, either great velocity or a fastball that has movement. You go with what brought you to the dance. Young pitchers, if they have no real fastball at every level that they play, they should concentrate more on just trying to find a college scholarship opportunity rather than believing they are going to be major league pitchers.

Anything can happen but the actual "Lightening in a Bottle" for being a major league pitcher is at a minimum, 1% or less.

Literally one in a million make it to the major leagues. That means that we have to prepare for college and another life if "WE" don't make it and the opportunity to have a sports scholarships, a free ride if the player is talented enough to play at that level. Remember, every level that you move up into brings more and more exceptionally talented players and legitimate stars to that level. Higher levels never have less or poorer talent.

Over the last 20 years or so there has been an explosion in Pitchers, specifically Mark the Bird Fidrych, Jeremy Bonderman, Dontrelle Willis, Mark Prior, Dice-K, Tim Lincecum, and El Duque and dozens of others, but these guys had success and were just starting to be legitimate stars until they lost it or were injured. Most lost it!!! What happened to all of this major league talent?

I want to explain what happened to most of these pitchers so you can avoid bad terminal issues for pitchers.

Some of these guys just plainly forgot what got them to the major leagues, developing bad habits, trying new pitches, developing bad pitches and arm movements and arm positions that were not part of their natural abilities and not being with good pitching coaches who were successful in the past. Allow me to make a huge point:

Pitchers who don't win in the Major Leagues most of the time are somehow, in the good old boys network, becoming pitching coaches with and for their major league friends. I have never understood why a guy who has had little or no success of note, winds up being pitching coaches and coaching the likes of Mark the Bird Fidrych, Jeremy Bonderman, Dontrelle Willis, Mark Prior, Dice-K, Tim Lincecum, and El Duque. How many of them could have had a hall of fame career if their coaching staffs had recognized the damage and bad habits somehow they picked up from some coach?

Do Airlines and or Doctors allow non-talented, unlicensed or unsuccessful pilots?

Of course not. We go to what we believe are the most talented successful professionals. We look at the professional's resumes and look at their success rates and what did they do to be good and successful.

The same thing can be said of a pitching coach. If he has not won in the major leagues, shown signs of success, or not had a good pitch that was a winning pitch and effective, how the heck can we expect this coach to be successful with the most talented arms and young careers.

I have always thought if a pitching coach has not had success in the major leagues how can you expect them to produce successful and great pitchers. Why did they not have success when they were playing? I am not talking about winning 20 every year, especially in this day and age, but at least consistent years of winning. For example, great pitchers have at least 5 year runs whereby the rule the game and win and win.

I do blame a lot of injuries on pitching coaches because they are supposed to first understand fundamentals. Why can't most of them understand or see the basics of keeping a pitcher healthy? Why are

we having a rash and seemingly a plague of injuries to young pitchers now?
There are numerous reasons but first the pitching coach must understand the fundamentals.
They should be able to identify the following issues and if they did we would have less injuries in the major leagues and other leagues.

These are the Four Fundamentals for every pitcher.

1) Pitchers must keep their Heads as "STILL" as possible. Just like a golfer, if the head moves playing golf, real bad things happen, as we all know.
2) Pitchers must stay in a "Groove". I define "Groove" as throwing the baseball from the same arm position time and time again. If you get out of the groove, pitches will start to do other things, will certainly effect your control, will make you rush your normal pitching groove and amongst other things, can start to contribute to arm injuries or worse, surgical procedures.
3) Wind-Up Issues. Is it too big, too much body movement, not landing consistently in the same area pitch after pitch?
4) LEGS: If a pitcher does not pitch with his legs he will never ever achieve his maximum fastball. You must learn how to "Push-Off" on the mound. You can use that Radar Gun all you want and the major league teams do play

with the Radar Gun. Most people that I have talked to have told me they will move the radar gun up, in home parks, in speed anywhere from 2 up to 6mph in order to get the crowd to scream, holler and really get excited trying to make the home team rally. The Radar Gun is the worst enemy for a young pitcher. Veterans don't pay attention to it, but new pitchers believe that they will be a star if they can break 100 time and time again and they don't realize that the Guns are being manipulated. Let me prove a point: How many pitchers in the major leagues throw the baseball at more than a 100 mph and are actually successful. Anyone?

5) <u>I contend NO ONE throws the baseball at 100.</u>

There have been some good and great pitching coaches. I will only talk about a couple good ones, I shall not name the bad ones. You can look at resumes and careers and see for yourself and then look at the success of the pitchers that they have coached and all of your questions will be answered.

The greatest pitching coach as far as resume and history was Johnny Sain. In fact he was so good at a stretch in his career when he was pitching on the same team as the great Warren Sphan, that there was a phrase coined for him and Sphan: "Sphan and Sain and Pray for Rain". They were a lethal and successful two-some. He was a star as a pitcher and learned the game and the application of his ability produced numerous 20 game winners and one 31 game winner.

His success with pitchers as far as the resume will show is second to no one. Sain not only could teach and manage your repertoire but also show you and prove to you with major league explanations how and why pitches do certain things and actually show you how these pitches can be helped and tossed. I closely follow the Art of Pitching as described and detailed for me by Johnny Sain.
Dave Duncan was another great coach and he was a major league catcher. He paid attention, and he learned the art of pitching from super pitchers like Catfish Hunter, Kenny Holtzman, Blue Moon Odom, Bob Gibson and others.
Art Fowler, as a pitching coach for many years for Billy Martin has terrific success and was a great teacher of how to throw curve balls and sliders.

If coaches and players uses horrible models and information or are trying to invent a new wheel for pitching mechanics and focus on the wrong areas of the delivery when instructing, then you will have a pitcher just never getting to his peak and quite possibly starting his way to injury. At all costs, I try never to allow one of our students to violate the 4 Fundamentals.

If a coaching staff is talking to you about Pumping Iron, length of your arm extension as you throw a pitch, throwing curve balls, throwing sliders; folks they are getting ready to prepare you for a very short career.

NO ONE below the age of 17 or 18 should ever throw a curve ball or slider. NO one at the age of 17 or 18 should attempt a curve or slider without the absolute assurance that the coaching staff is known to be successful and why were they successful and they actually know how to throw a curveball or slider with proof.
Keep in mind, at the High School Level most pitchers win because they have terrific young fastballs. If you have to throw more than 5% or so of change-ups or other trick pitches, please keep in mind that your focus must be on college and not major league baseball. There is nothing that compares to a great fastball, NOTHING!!!

PROPER FUNDAMENTALS will give you an opportunity to play for a long time, but sooner or later we all are injured in some form or we lose some of our talent unique to us and only us. But by the time we start to lose our fastballs we have learned tons about pitching and keeping hitters off balance and at that point we have learned how to throw a real curve ball and a real slider or other pitches that require abnormal and dangerous ways to jeopardize your arm. We then have accepted the risk. You don't learn how to pitch, actually "pitch" until you start to lose something on your fastball. It is always great to be working on a new pitch, but pitchers can't just screw around with pitches and they should always have a reason as to why you are throwing a baseball.

If you want to play long term...
If you want to play to win...
If you want to play at your best for maybe a couple decades:
Your focus and all of your training should be in the Fundamentals of pitching. They work and have worked for more than 100 years.

Jeremy Bonderman, Dontelle Willis, Mark Prior, Dice-K, Lincecum and El Duque, Mark the Bird, and dozens of others were never given good help with the basics and fundamentals and information on pitching from good, credible and substantial successful professionals. These short runs for stardom by these stars were terribly misinformed or the coaching staffs had no idea why these guys were having issues. Why did these staffs not see the actual fundamental errors and let their stars develop bad habits?
After all, these pitchers truly trusted and relied upon these professional pitching staffs.
My message to all who are looking to go to colleges for pitching assistance and knowledge; first see what kinds of success these schools had, why they had the success they had, did any of those pitching staffs have guys that made it to any levels in professional baseball and of course major league baseball. What is the philosophy of the manager and pitching coaches when it comes to breaking balls?
Start with their coach's resumes and former players. References are always a great way to start a search for anything, but keep in mind, we must protect ourselves

first. History and results will make you go in the right direction and at least in the beginning of your college career you will know that your coaching staff is the best and has produced winners and great pitchers.

Other Books By Denny McLain

I Told You I Wasn't Perfect

"31-6"

Denny McLain

ABOUT THE AUTHOR

Denny McLain is native to the Chicago area, born in Markham and attended Mt Carmel High where he played sports, excelling at baseball at both short stop and pitcher. In those early days he also met his future wife Sharon Boudreau, daughter of baseball Royalty Lou Boudreau, a Hall of Fame player with Cleveland.

McLain played at the major league level for 10 years, becoming a legend for the Detroit Tigers. In 1968 the Tigers won the World Series and McLain became the last player in the majors to win 30 or more games in one season (31-6). Only 11 players have done this in the 20th century.

From the time he was drafted from high school, McLain was brash, outspoken and always controversial. Most of the time he backed up his bragging, but he often got into hot water anyhow. His first pro game after signing with the Chicago White Sox resulted in a no hitter and striking out 16 batters. The White Sox sold him to Detroit and he worked his way up from the minors in quick order. Starting as a relief pitcher he established himself as a contender for the starting rotation by striking out seven batters in a row after coming into a game to relieve Dave Wickersham. He ended the season 16-6, a 2.61 ERA and 192 strikeouts. Only Sam McDowell and Mickey Lolich were ahead of him in strikeouts.

In 1966 he started in the All Star Game with a record of 13-4 and retired all nine batters in just 28 pitches, a true perfect exhibition of pitching.

In 1967 McLain's life changed as his bragging, loud mouthed, cocky ways ran head on into Johnny Sain, Detroit's new pitching coach. It was Sain, McLain admits, who finally taught him to pitch and pitch properly. Here Denny learned The Art of Pitching from the master. He finished 1967 at 17-16 and was winless after August 29th. He had injured his foot severely and likely cost the Tigers the Pennant in 1967.

Trying to finally win the World Series, the Tigers attempted without success to move both McLain and Al Kaline in the off season. Fortunately for Detroit they failed.

Denny and the Tigers hit 1968 hard, winning nine in a row after dropping the opener. McLain was on fire, winning at a remarkable pace. The Tigers were also winning on days Denny did not pitch and the combination pushed the team to the top of the division. On Sept 10th McLain won his astounding 29th game. He won number 30 on a national TV hook up on Sept 14, beating Oakland 5-4. Dizzy Dean, the last man to win 30 games for the Cardinals, was there to celebrate the victory.

It is said that after the Tigers clinched the pennant, McLain offered up a soft pitch to his long time idol, New York's Mickey Mantle. Mantle needed just one more homer to pass Jimmie Fox on the All Time Home Run list. The Tigers were ahead 6-1 in the eighth inning and McLain threw one to Mantle, who blasted it into the seats, no small feat in any game. As Mantle rounded the bases he tipped his hat to Denny. Denny denies to this day that he gave up a run to Mantle. "Are you crazy? Give one to Mantle? He would hit it to Canada if someone was foolish enough to do that," says Denny with a smile. McLain was officially reprimanded by Major League Baseball Commissioner William Eckert.

Long a musical protégée (he earned a degree in music), McLain endorsed Hammond Organs and Pepsi in the off season and appeared on many TV shows like *Ed Sullivan*, *Steve Allen*, *What's My Line*, and *The Joey Bishop Show*. He even recorded two albums for Capitol Records; *Denny McLain at The Organ* and *Denny McLain in Las Vegas*.

In January 1969 McLain was selected as the Associated Press Male Athlete of The Year.

In five years Denny won:

108 wins

55 in 2 years

ERA in 1968 1.96

280 strike outs

Won 24 games 1969 and won second CY YOUNG AWARD

Currently Denny visits and performs at many charity events, especially with the USA MILITARY ALL STARS, a team of active duty soldiers originally commissioned by President George Bush 41 in 1989. He lives in Michigan.

# The Art Of Pitching

www.ingramcontent.com/pod-product-compliance
Lightning Source LLC
Chambersburg PA
CBHW071314040426
42444CB00009B/2015